EARTH'S WILD WINDS

SANDRA FRIEND

TWENTY-FIRST CENTURY BOOKS
BROOKFIELD, CONNECTICUT

**TO MY BROTHER SCOTT, WHO KNOWS
THE DANGER OF A WICKED WIND**

Published by Twenty-First Century Books
A Division of The Millbrook Press, Inc.
2 Old New Milford Road
Brookfield, Connecticut 06804
www.millbrookpress.com

Library of Congress Cataloging-in-Publication Data
Friend, Sandra.
Earth's wild winds / Sandra Friend.
p. cm. — (Exploring planet earth)
Includes bibliographical references and index.
Summary: Examines different aspects of the wind, including its measurement,
effects on weather, potential destructiveness, and uses.
ISBN 0-7613-2673-1 (lib. bdg.)
1. Winds—Juvenile literature. [1. Winds.] I. Title.
QC931.4 .F75 2002 551.51'8—dc21 2001006515

Cover photographs courtesy of Visuals Unlimited (© R. F. Myers) and Photo Researchers, Inc. (© Jack Fields)
Photographs courtesy of Photo Researchers, Inc.: pp. 4 (© Pat & Tom Leeson), 8 (top © Jules Bucher; bottom
© Charles D. Winters) 10 (© David Parker/SPL), 27 (© Larry Miller), 32 (© NOAA), 41 (© Wayne Lawler),
44 (© David Muerdter), 48 (© John Mead/SPL), 49 (© Sylvain Cazenave); NGS Image Collection: p. 7 (©
Michael Nichols); North Wind Picture Archives: p. 13; PhotoEdit: p. 21 (© Tom McCarthy); NOAA/
Department of Commerce: pp. 22 (Commander John Bortniak), 24 (George E. Marsh Album), 53 (Historic
NWS Collection); National Center for Atmospheric Research/University Corporation for Atmospheric
Research/National Science Foundation: pp. 29, 35; Visuals Unlimited: p. 36 (© William J. Weber); NASA:
pp. 37, 38; Photri, Inc.: p. 51; Corbis: p. 52 (© Wolfgang Kaehler)

Illustrations courtesy of Sharon Lane Holm

Quotation on page 47 from *Yak Butter and Black Tea: A Journey Into Tibet*
by Wade Brackenbury. Copyright © 1997 by the author.
Reprinted by permission of Algonquin Books of Chapel Hill,
a division of Workman Publishing.

CONTENTS

PREFACE

Aloft on a rising thermal, an eagle hovers in a fixed position over a lake, watching for a fish to break to the surface.

The unfurled sails of a sailboat catch the wind, billowing out in huge crescents, propelling the boat out into the sun-splashed waters of a bay.

Trees bend and branches snap as a strong gust rips through a dense forest.

We can't see the wind, and yet it communicates. It brings us sounds, smells, and sensations. We feel the power of a sudden burst of wind as empty trash cans tumble down the street. We listen to tree branches creak and groan as they snap back and forth, strained by the movement of the wind. We hear wind whistling in the power lines, making ghostly noises in the night. We smell the stench when a red tide scours the shoreline, the sea breeze thick with the odor of dying fish.

Sometimes the wind does more than communicate. It carries. Pollen drifts across the prairie. Salt covers the metallic sheen of cars parked close to the sea. A sandstorm roars across the Sahara, scouring everything in its path. The wild winds of a hurricane grab and tear apart houses, pluck trees from the ground, and force pine needles through concrete walls. Violent tornadoes pick up and drop heavy objects—houses, cars, livestock, and even people.

From gentle breezes to furious attacks, mild and wild, the earth's winds are with us every day. We have no control over their force, but we can learn to respect the wind and to live with what it brings us each day.

1
UNDERSTANDING THE WIND

In the mid-1950s, a forest ranger walking the open range in the Carlsbad Caverns National Park in New Mexico came across a very different kind of cave opening. It made noise! It screamed and howled like a banshee.

He noted the phenomenon in a report. It was forgotten until 1986, when a group of cavers from Colorado received permission from the National Park Service to explore the cave. Climbing down nearly 90 feet (27 meters) into the sinkhole entrance to the cave, they felt a strong wind rising from loose stones in the bottom of the sinkhole. Removing the stones, they found a small hole where wind emerged with gusts of up to 50 miles (80 kilometers) per hour.

After two years of digging, they broke into one of the world's greatest underground wonders—Lechuguilla Cave. With more than 100 miles (161 kilometers) of mapped passageways and 1,567 feet (478 meters) of depth, Lechuguilla is the deepest limestone cave in the United States, the fifth longest in the world—and one of the world's windiest.

WINDS OF MYTH AND LEGEND

Because the wind is always with us, we have always sought to understand where it comes from. The ancient Greeks believed that all of the world's winds blew out from the insides of caves. The Greek god of wind, Aeolus, kept the winds locked up in the caves of the Lipari Islands, in the Mediterranean Sea. Aeolus would allow winds to escape at different times of the year, causing changes in the weather.

As recently as 350 B.C., the Greek philosopher Aristotle described wind as a force rising from inside the earth. But fifty years later, another Greek philosopher, Theophrastus, wrote the *Book of Signs*, a book on wind. Collecting together folklore and wise sayings related to wind, he challenged the theory that wind came from within the earth. Theophrastus said that winds came from every direction— north, south, east, west, and all points in between. He assigned a special name to each of the winds.

The ancient Chinese thought that wind came from the skies, where the dragon god Fei Lein beat his wings to stir up the atmosphere, bringing not just fierce winds but thunderstorms. In India, the Hindus credited Rudra, a god of storms and wind, with bringing the stinging gusts that came with cyclones. The sailors of stormy Finland would implore the god Ilmarinen for good weather. "You can raise the wind, you can calm the storm. Give us good wind, spare us from your tempest."

Myths and legends helped people to explain the wind. But to understand the wind, they needed to start measuring it. Where did it come from? How fast was it going?

Lechuguilla Cave: Winds blow out of caves because of a difference in the barometric pressure between the surface and the cave. As the outside air pressure falls, air inside the cave blows out. When the outside pressure rises, the cave sucks air in. When explorers find a cave with wind pouring out of it, they can use the wind speed to estimate how extensive that cave might be.

MEASURING THE WIND

The earliest efforts to measure the wind were simple. Wet a finger and hold it up in the air. Watch how the trees sway. Tie a piece of cloth to a tree and see which way it flaps in the breeze. The world's first wind vanes (or weather vanes), simple devices that showed from which direction the wind was blowing, date back to ancient Egypt and China. From Norway to Rome, most cultures developed traditional weather vanes, which changed little in form over the centuries.

Above: an anemometer connected electrically to a remote dial. Below: a copper weathervane

Meteorology, the science of weather, began in 1450 when Italian architect Leon Battista Alberti invented a device for measuring wind speed. The anemometer is made up of four hemispherical cups at the ends of a shaft that rotates around a center pole. As the wind grows stronger, the cups rotate faster, and their movement is measured to calculate the wind speed. In 1643, Evangelista Torricelli invented the barometer. The barometer measures the rise and fall of air pressure, which is the difference in the density of molecules as air is heated and cooled. A barometer indicates that a change in the weather is on the way.

In the early 1800s, the anemometer was still just a scientific tool. A person on the street would rely on simple observation to guess at the wind speed. In 1805, Rear Admiral Sir Francis Beaufort of the Royal (British) Navy created the Beaufort Wind Scale, used to determine wind speed based on watching what the wind was doing to the natural environment.

When scientist Blaise Pascal carried a barometer to the top of a mountain in 1648, he discovered that air pressure was lower at higher elevations. Although the invention of the hot-air balloon in 1783 was for sport, scientists quickly seized on its potential for measuring air at high elevations. In 1785, Dr. John Jeffries took the first-ever scientific measurements of temperature, humidity, and barometric pressure at altitudes up to 9,000 feet (2,740 meters), struggling along in a leaky balloon with Jean Pierre Blanchard. To reduce weight, the men had to strip to their underwear!

Unmanned weather balloons became the measuring tool of choice, carrying instruments aloft. They had to be reeled back in on a long string. In 1919, a group of German scientists sent a research kite 31,955 feet (9,740 meters) into the atmosphere! By the 1920s, a device called the radiosonde became the primary tool

BEAUFORT CHART

BEAUFORT NUMBER	WIND SPEED		DESCRIPTION	AIR MOTION	WATER MOTION
	MILES PER HOUR	KNOTS			
0	less than 1	less than 1	Calm	Smoke rises vertically	Smooth as a mirror
1	1–3	1–3	Light air	Smoke drifts	Slight ripples
2	4–7	4–6	Light breeze	Leaves rustle	Small, short wavelets
3	8–12	7–10	Gentle breeze	Leaves and twigs in constant motion	Large wavelets, breaking crests
4	13–18	11–16	Moderate	Small branches move	Small waves, some white caps
5	19–24	17–21	Fresh	Small trees sway	Moderate waves, many whitecaps
6	25–31	22–27	Strong	Large branches sway	Large waves, whitecaps, and spray
7	32–38	28–33	Near gale	Whole trees sway	Sea heaps up, white foam blows
8	39–46	34–40	Gale	Twigs break off trees	Moderately high long waves, well-marked streaks of foam
9	47–54	41–47	Strong gale	Branches break off trees	High waves, rolling seas, dense foam
10	55–63	48–55	Storm	Trees uprooted	Large waves with over-hanging crests, sea white with foam
11	64–72	56–63	Violent storm	Widespread damage	Waves over 18 feet (6m), reduced visibility
12	73 or more	64–71	Hurricane	Disaster	Waves over 42 feet (14m), minimal visibility

A spherical-shaped "Jimsphere" weather balloon is more stable in flight than flexible balloons.

for sampling the atmosphere. Carried aloft by balloons, the radiosonde gathers and transmits basic information on barometric pressure, temperature, and humidity.

A NATURAL ENGINE

By gathering information about the way the wind behaved, scientists could theorize what caused wind. In 1661, Edmund Halley, the scientist who discovered Halley's comet, concluded that the movement of the wind came from "the Action of the Sun's Beams upon the Air and Water, as he passes every day over the Oceans, considered together with the nature of the Soyl." Halley understood that sunlight's effect on the surface of the earth was crucial for the production of wind and that air was expanded by heat. Fifty years later George Hadley, a London lawyer, added information on how the earth's rotation affects the creation of wind. The research of countless scientists and meteorologists contributed to what we know now about wind.

All wind starts as air. The earth's atmosphere wraps us in a blanket of air, providing the special mix of elements that we need to be able to breathe. When the air starts moving, we feel the wind.

The earth, the sun, and our atmosphere work together like a giant engine, generating wind and weather. As sunlight reaches the earth, it passes along its heat in a process called conduction. Every surface that the sunlight reaches stores its warmth as energy. Filled with energy, the mole-

METEOROLOGY TODAY

Today's meteorologists answer the same basic questions about wind as scientists have through history, but they use cool tools to predict problems that can happen when wicked winds kick up. Although the original design of the anemometer is still used by weather stations today, a new sonic anemometer determines wind speed more accurately by measuring the changes in sound waves sent between two fixed points. New Sonic Detection and Ranging Devices (SODAR) make high-pitched chirping sounds that are reflected back to the device, allowing the wind speed and direction to be measured by the differences in the echoes. Doppler SODAR creates a three-dimensional graphic of the wind. These devices are used for weather research, for planning evacuation routes in case of an emergency, and for pinpointing problems at airports caused by wind shear and ground turbulence on runways.

Twice every day, at midnight and noon, the National Weather Service in the United States launches hundreds of radiosonde balloons into the atmosphere. These balloons can drift as high as 100,000 feet (30,480 meters). Each carries a rawindsonde, a rigid cardboard tube containing sensors and electronics that measure the changes in temperature, pressure, and water vapor at different altitudes and transmit the readings back to a ground station.

Meteorologists also rely on feedback from aircraft sent into storms. In aircraft adapted specifically to collect data from hurricanes, the information is received directly by measuring devices on the aircraft, including Doppler radar that maps the flow of the wind. More often, aircraft launch a dropwindsonde, a version of the rawindsonde that transmits data back to the aircraft and can be tracked by the airplane's radar.

cules that make up the roof of a house, the still waters of a pond, and the rocks in your yard start bouncing around. All of these surfaces release their excess energy as heat, which warms the air around them. Warm air weighs less than cold air, since the molecules are spread out more thinly. So the warm air rises, and the heavier, denser cold air sinks down into the space created as the warm air moves. This perpetual cycle of convection, where heated air rises and cold air sinks, creates wind.

Thanks to weather, landscape, and the uniqueness of the earth's atmosphere, the engine isn't precisely tuned. Overcast skies in one region mean less sunlight striking the ground. Some surfaces, like the massive sand dunes of the Sahara Desert, soak up more sunlight than other surfaces. And our atmosphere, made up of five different layers of air in five very different temperature zones, fuels the movement of wind by the exchange of heat and cold as air rises and sinks.

Across the surface of our planet, air undergoes convection within a circulation cell. At both the North Pole and the South Pole, cold air sinks and flows away from the poles, returning to them as warm air. At the equator, warm air rises and flows away from the equator, returning to it as cold air. A third circular motion of winds occurs between these two cells. This giant convection system is also called a "Hadley cell," in honor of George Hadley, who first described this natural engine of winds.

Within this engine, enormous amounts of energy are created and dispersed. Winds push clouds across the sky, often moving whole storm systems across a continent in a few days, carrying moisture picked up over one country to rain down on another. Winds loft pollutants from one city to another, moving smokestack emissions from midwestern factories to New England in a day. Winds spread the ash from volcanic eruptions around the entire planet, enabling the emissions from a single volcano (like Mount Pinatubo in the Philippines) to affect the earth's weather for years. On a smaller scale, wind scatters seeds, spreads pollen, smoothes out fresh-fallen snow, lifts kites into the sky, and provides cool breezes on a hot day.

2
A WORLD WRAPPED IN WIND

"The Admiral here says 'this headwind was very necessary to me, for my crew had grown much alarmed, dreading that they never should meet in these seas with a fair wind to return to Spain.'"—September 22, 1492

"We set sail about ten o'clock, with the wind southeast and stood southerly for the island I mentioned above, which is a very large one, and where according to the account of the natives on board, there is much gold, the inhabitants wearing it in bracelets upon their arms, legs, and necks, as well as in their ears and at their noses."—October 15, 1492

The journal of Christopher Columbus reflects the everyday importance of wind on a sailor's voyage, especially a voyage of such magnitude as crossing the Atlantic Ocean. Understanding the wind was important to early sailors, who wanted to figure out not just how to get to a certain point of land—but how to come home, too!

UNDER PRESSURE

While the heating of the earth's surface by the sun drives the engine that creates wind, the reason the wind blows in so many directions is due to differences in air pressure in the atmosphere.

When you pump up a bicycle tire, you create higher pressure in the tire than is in the surrounding atmosphere. While this pressure cushions your ride, it also sets up an imbalance between the inside of the tire and the air around your bicycle. You end up pumping up the bicycle tire again and again because the air inside the tire slowly leaks out to bring the pressure into balance.

The same thing happens with air in the atmosphere. To equalize pressure, air under high pressure moves to areas of lower pressure. As air moves from one place in the atmosphere to another, it creates wind.

As air cools down, its molecules huddle close together, making it denser. It sinks. Dense, cooling air, dropping down toward the earth's surface, creates areas of high pressure, or highs, in the atmosphere.

A high-pressure system rotates as it flows toward the nearest area of low pressure, thanks to the Coriolis force caused by the rotation of the earth. It's the same force that makes water flow counterclockwise down a drain in the Northern Hemisphere and clockwise in the Southern Hemisphere. Since air is also fluid, the Coriolis force affects it—pushing it to the right of the direction of motion in the Northern Hemisphere and to the left in the Southern Hemisphere.

Whirling air masses, islands of static air, spin off the region where winds collide. They rotate clockwise away from the turbulence, picking up speed and moisture as they move away from areas of high pressure. An air mass can cover millions of square miles. As the air mass sits over a large body of land or water, it slowly adapts to the temperature of the surface below it. Air masses transfer heat to different parts of the atmosphere by either cooling down (radiating heat) or warming up (absorbing heat) until they reach the same temperature as the surface.

When air warms up, its molecules spread out, making it lighter. It rises. As rising air squeezes between areas of high pressure, it forms a low-pressure system, or low. Air spirals inward in a counterclockwise pattern. Once the low-pressure system breaks free from the turmoil between two air masses, it spins away and moves through the atmosphere. Low-pressure systems are generally responsible for the world's worst winds—hurricanes, typhoons, cyclones, and tornadoes.

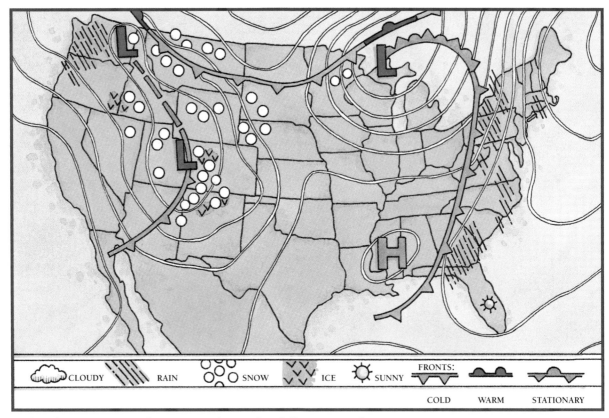

Isobar lines on a weather map indicate the differences in barometric pressure between regions.

As the contour lines on a map of a mountain show the difference in altitude, the isobar lines on a weather map show the difference in pressure between regions, as measured in millibars by a barometer. Measurements below 1,000 millibars indicate low pressure. Measurements over 1,000 millibars indicate high pressure.

ATMOSPHERIC CURRENTS

Most human activity takes place in the lowest two layers of the atmosphere, the stratosphere and the troposphere. In these layers, there are predictable currents of air, known winds that we rely on every day. Meteorologists study them to predict the weather. Airline pilots take them into considera-

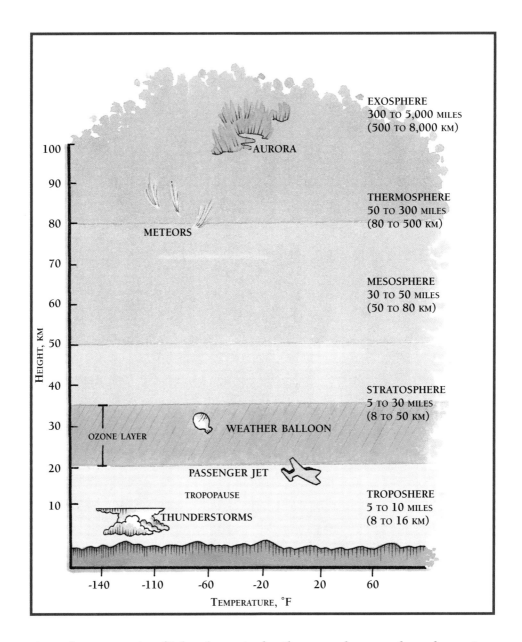

EXOSPHERE
300 TO 5,000 MILES
(500 TO 8,000 KM)

AURORA

THERMOSPHERE
50 TO 300 MILES
(80 TO 500 KM)

METEORS

MESOSPHERE
30 TO 50 MILES
(50 TO 80 KM)

STRATOSPHERE
5 TO 30 MILES
(8 TO 50 KM)

OZONE LAYER

WEATHER BALLOON

PASSENGER JET

TROPOPAUSE

TROPOSHERE
5 TO 10 MILES
(8 TO 16 KM)

THUNDERSTORMS

HEIGHT, KM

100
90
80
70
60
50
40
30
20
10

-140   -110   -60   -20   20   60

TEMPERATURE, °F

tion when preparing flight plans. And sailors use them to chart the easiest course across open water.

More than 5 miles (8 kilometers) above us, in the stratosphere, the winds consistently move from west to east. Known as prevailing **westerlies**, these winds flow across both hemispheres, in rhythm with the rotation of the earth. They move in gigantic waves, with lengths of more than

4,000 miles (6,440 kilometers) and heights of around 550 miles (885 kilometers). The winds of the stratosphere are relatively stable and predictable. On an airplane, climbing through clouds, the captain may take the plane up higher to avoid turbulence. As the plane rises, it bursts through the top of the clouds into sunshine. Most commercial aircraft fly in the stratosphere to avoid turbulence and bad weather.

The **jet stream** is a unique and powerful westerly wind in the stratosphere. It was discovered by a squadron of U.S. Air Force B-29 bombers flying west to attack Japan in World War II. Flying higher than any other aircraft had before, they struggled against unexpectedly fierce head winds. Sharp differences in the temperature of the air in the atmosphere fuels the jet stream, which can flow at speeds up to 250 miles (412 kilometers) per hour in the winter. The jet stream acts like a river of air, throwing waves of wind off its edges.

In the troposphere, there are three general categories of wind. **Persistent winds** wrap the planet in an unending ribbon of air movement. **Local persistent winds** behave in predictable ways, but are limited to certain parts of the world. **Episodic winds** occur on a seasonal basis, but can be unpredictable, irregular, and fearsome. They include monsoons, cyclones, hurricanes, and tornadoes.

TACKLING THE TRADES

Phoenician sailors of the seventh century B.C. learned the winds well enough to create trade routes to the islands of Greece, and to leave the Mediterranean for the Atlantic Ocean, where they sailed north to the British Isles and south to Africa, founding colonies. By the fifth century B.C., Greek sailors plied the waters to Egypt, returning home when the episodic **meltemi** wind changed direction. Meanwhile, Arabian and Chinese sailors discovered the **monsoon**, an episodic wind that spends half the year blowing northeast and half the year blowing southwest. From the Arabic word *mavism*, meaning "season," the monsoon winds led Arab sailors to the Malabar Coast of India, where they established the spice trade.

In the late 1400s, Portuguese sailors discovered that they could follow an eastern flow of wind across the Atlantic and then maneuver their ships toward the northwest to catch a westerly wind home. Treated as a state secret shared only with Spain, this discovery led to the great voyages of Vasco da Gama and Christopher Columbus. But by 1661, Edmund Halley had created the world's first map of these winds, the **trade winds**—winds that flow steadily toward regions of low pressure near the equator. The winds blow from a northeastern direction in the Northern Hemisphere and a southeastern direction in the Southern Hemisphere. The secret was out. Sailors quickly put it to use to explore the world.

PERSISTENT WINDS

The trade winds are **easterlies**, with a tendency to blow from east to west. In tropical latitudes, these winds can be strong and persistent. Easterlies also occur over the Arctic and Antarctic as **polar easterlies**, blasts of cold air spun away from the poles by the Coriolis force.

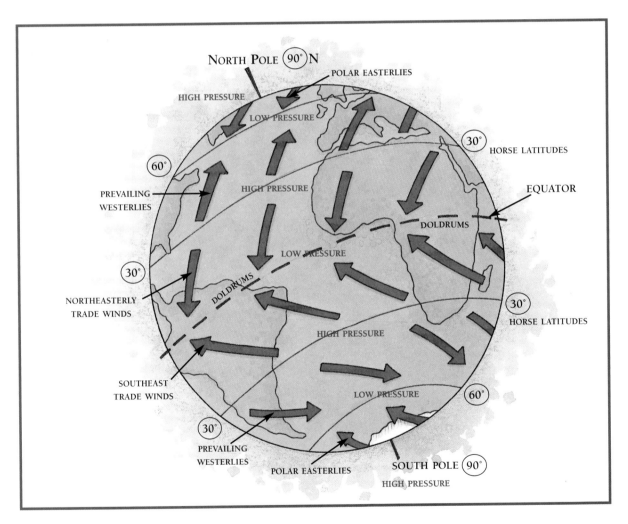

BECALMED

"The sea being smooth and tranquil, the sailors murmured, saying that they had got into smooth water, where it would never blow to carry them back to Spain; but afterwards the sea rose without wind, which astonished them."—September 23, 1492

Christopher Columbus experienced a fearful moment on his journey in the **doldrums**, one of the two areas of the Atlantic Ocean where winds could sometimes simply stop blowing. The doldrums form where the trade winds of the Northern and Southern Hemisphere meet, causing areas of low barometric pressure with no wind. Stuck in the calm of the doldrums, a sailing ship could drift for days on mirror-smooth seas. Food and water supplies could drop to dangerous levels as sailors waited for some wind, any wind, to push them onward in their journey.

Similarly, winds in the horse latitudes could stall a ship. In this high-pressure region between the trade winds and the westerlies, under blistering heat about 30 degrees from the equator, food supplies would dwindle while ships waited for a change in wind direction. These latitudes were named for the plight of the horses aboard the ship, since as starving horses overheated and died, sailors would dump them overboard.

Dutch sailors discovered that once they rounded the Cape of Good Hope at the tip of Africa, they could rely on the Roaring Forties—easterly strong winds between latitudes of 40 and 50 degrees south—to get to Indonesia and Australia. Between 50 and 60 degrees south are the Furious Fifties. The Screaming Sixties lie south of 60 degrees latitude south, tearing west through Drake's Passage between Antarctica and the tip of South America at Cape Horn. Australia was one of the last continents discovered by Europeans because of these fierce belts of winds surrounding it.

The earth's strongest persistent winds are the westerlies. In both hemispheres, they generate whirling cells of high-pressure and low-pressure winds, fueling worldwide weather patterns. Especially in winter, westerlies reach speeds as high as 70 miles (113 kilometers) per hour. When they roar over the ocean, they can create wind-driven waves more than 50 feet (15 meters) high.

3
BACKYARD BREEZES

While trade winds, easterlies, and westerlies affect the entire planet, many other persistent winds occur in much smaller spaces—such as beaches along a wide expanse of ocean or the steep leeward side of a tall mountain.

Called local persistent winds, these winds fall into several categories: sea and land breezes, mountain and valley winds, and seasonal regional winds. Within these categories, there are more than 150 specific local winds, each tied to a region of the earth. The interaction between wind and landscape plays a major role in the formation of weather and climate.

LIGHT AND BREEZY

Gentle, calming **land breezes** and **sea breezes** occur because of the difference in temperature between the surface of the water and the surface of the land. Like the tides, winds continually flow back and forth between the two surfaces. During the day, the land heats up under the sun, and the air above it rises, allowing cool air to flow in off the sea to take its place. At night, the air over the sea is warmer, so it rises, allowing the cool air to flow out off the land and over the water. Sea breezes are so predictable and persistent that they can sculpt trees into unusual shapes, with branches pointing in the direction of the prevailing wind.

In regions close to the equator, such as the islands of the Caribbean, sea breezes occur year-round. In northerly climates, sea breezes tend to occur

Palm trees on a Florida beach blow in the wind.

mainly in spring and summer, when there is more of a difference in temperature between the land and the sea. Sea breezes occur over bodies of freshwater, too, such as the Great Lakes. The wind-sculpted pines of Killarney, in Northern Ontario, attest to the persistent easterly breezes that flow off Lake Huron.

SHAPED BY LANDSCAPE

In the White Mountains of New Hampshire, winds rise up a valley created by a tributary of the Connecticut River, drawn toward an area of permanent low pressure over Mount Washington. As the winds flow through this natural wind tunnel, they move like waves through mountain notches—

This cloud over an Alaska mountain peak was formed by orographic lifting.

producing a moment of eerie calm followed by a blast of howling wind. This wind is an **orographic** wind, shaped by landscape.

Orographic winds are some of the world's strongest winds. They can pour over mountain slopes like whitewater rapids, creating pools and eddies of air that behave in strange, dangerous ways. Mount Washington has the world's most consistently wicked winds, with frequent gusts of more than 100 miles (161 kilometers) per hour. Although Mount Washington is only 6,288 feet (1,917 meters) high—much lower than the peaks of the Rockies, the Alps, and the Himalayas—it sits at a spot where three major pathways of wind converge. According to the Bernoulli principle, wind in motion is always at lower pressure than stationary air, and will pull stationary air toward it. At Mount Washington, the Bernoulli effect causes extreme winds—including a world record burst of 231 miles (372 kilometers) per hour on April 12, 1934.

Mountain and valley landscapes create special conditions for these very localized winds. As rocky ridges above a valley absorb sunlight in the morning, convection creates rising currents of hot air, warmer than the air at the same altitude out over the valley. To replace the air, cooler, heavier air presses down, squeezing air up from the valley floor to the level of the rocky ridges, where that air also becomes heated and rises—causing a **thermal slope** wind. At night, the exposed rocks cool quickly, but the valley does not. The wind reverses direction.

In deep valleys, winds move from the wide end of the valley to the narrow end. These **lateral** winds can be strong and persistent enough to erode rocks and bend trees in a particular direction.

When wind hits a mountain, it drops its load of moisture on the windward side, leaving nothing but warm, parched air to flow over the leeward side of the mountain and into the valleys below. In the state of Washington, the windward side of the Cascade Range receives enormous amounts of rainfall, creating temperate rain forests. The leeward side is dry and desert-like. Winds that shape these environments are called **transmountain** winds.

'TIS THE SEASON

Seasonal winds occur only during certain parts of the year. In January and February, the **chinook** ("snow-eater") pours off the Rocky Mountains and into the Great Plains, raising temperatures suddenly and clearing away snow. On January 22, 1943, a chinook raised temperatures in Spearfish, South Dakota, from -4°F to 45°F (-20°C to 7°C) in just two minutes, cracking glass windows and plates! Similarly, the **foehn** of Switzerland swoops down from the Alps, clearing snow from its path. Both winds are **downslope** winds—warm, dry orographic winds given their strength by the shape of the mountains. Because of their immense height, the Rockies and the Alps act like boulders in a streambed of air, breaking the wind into whirling ripples and eddies, forced upward by the peaks and then flowing down into lower elevations, warmed by compression. There are many warm downslope winds across the world, occurring in different seasons and different places. They include the **Santa Ana** of California, the **zonda** of Argentina, the **koembang** in Java, and many others. Grouped together, they are called the **adiabatic** winds. The Santa Ana is so dry and hot that it draws the moisture out of plants, setting the stage for dangerous wildfires in the chaparral of the San Gabriel Mountains. The winds make it difficult to fight fires once they get started.

The end of winter signals the bitter **bora**. Roaring out of the Russian plains, it rakes across the Balkans, stirring the waves of the Adriatic Sea into foam. It flows like a waterfall, draining the high cold plateaus of Hungary into the warm coastal plains of Slovenia, Albania, and Greece. The cold, dry winds of the **mistral** drain the high plateau of Central France into the Rhone Valley and across to Provence. According to the Greek geographer Strabo, the fierce mistral "displaces rocks, hurls men from their chariots . . . and strips them of their clothes." These cold, dense winds, along with their many counterparts around the world, are called **katabatic** winds. Pulled by gravity, cold heavy air spills off high plateaus at high velocity, reaching speeds of up to 85 miles (137 kilometers) per hour.

Other winds follow seasonal movements of low pressure. Born in the deserts south of the Mediterranean Sea, the **sirocco** blows northward in the spring, irritating the countries and islands of the Mediterranean with hot,

A dust storm approaches Stratford, Texas, in 1935.

dry winds and sandstorms. Scooped up by the wind, Sahara sands fall as red rain on distant shores. The easterly **levant** brings foggy, rainy weather to the Mediterranean during the winter, while the **maestro** carries clear skies as it blows northwesterly across the Adriatic Sea in the summertime. Immense walls of dust and sand, up to 3,000 feet (914 meters) high, are carried by the **haboob** (Arabic for "phenomena"), which roars at up to 50 miles (80 kilometers) per hour across the deserts of the United States, Egypt, and Sudan during the summer months. A **nor'easter** brings chilly, damp, and sometimes snowy weather to New England in the winter, driving cold, wet winds inland from the North Atlantic. The **norther** pushes bitter, dry polar air from Canada down through the central plains of the United States in the winter. Temperatures can drop up to 25 degrees Fahrenheit (-30 degrees Celsius) an hour, or 50 degrees Fahrenheit (10 degrees Celsius) in a day, all the way to the Gulf of Mexico.

AN ILL WIND

Some winds can cause people to become ill or depressed. When the Santa Ana roars into Los Angeles, the humidity drops and the air becomes crisp and dry—causing bloody noses, sinus troubles, and headaches. The residents of Tangier, Morocco, blame their headaches on the levant. The dry winds of the sirocco cause cracked lips and skin, making people nervous and depressed. In the fourteenth century A.D., murderers were dealt with more leniently by the Ottoman Empire if the murder occurred during the sirocco. The oppressive winds of the foehn can bring on irritability. "It renders the brain torpid, robs a person of his appetite, and seems to bloat up the entire body," said a French observer in 1684.

4 WHIRLING, SWIRLING WINDS

When leaves twirl around and around in a circle and dance down the sidewalk, they are caught up in one of the earth's tiniest bits of weather—a **dust whirl**. A spot of ground warms up, heated by the sun. The air above the spot is cooler, so convection occurs on a tiny scale, creating a miniature disturbance. These little whirlwinds develop from the ground up. As the warm air rises, it spins—thanks to the Coriolis effect, which puts a spin on everything as the earth whirls through space.

DANCING, PRANCING WINDS

The desert on a hot summer afternoon provides the perfect birthplace for a much larger type of spinning wind—the **dust devil**. Dust devils typically form in the afternoon, after the ground heats up, warming the air above it. When the warmed air begins to rise, it expands and begins to swirl. It quickly picks up momentum, sucking up dirt, sand, leaves, and other debris, moving across the ground.

Dust devils can range in size from a few feet to more than 300 feet (91 meters) across and often rise 100 feet (30 meters) high. They travel only a few miles per hour, so they rarely cause destruction. Although most dust devils last only a few minutes, some can rival the size and duration of tornadoes—one reported over the Bonneville Salt Flats in Utah traveled more than 40 miles (64 kilometers) and rose up to 24,500 feet (7,468 meters)! Although dust devils can happen anywhere—it takes just sunshine and dry

Dust devils like this are common in Kansas.

ground to get convection going—the most spectacular and most frequent displays of whirling dust happen in the deserts of the United States, Africa, the Arabian Peninsula, and Australia.

In Australia, dust devils are called **willy-willys**. Dozens can form at the same time on hot, cloudless days, dancing in place. Dust devils also appear over frozen, snow-covered ground, picking up glistening flakes of snow, creating what looks like a white tornado.

Whirlwinds, swirling columns of heated air caused by convection, typically rise from the ground up. But atmospheric whirlwinds can form around the edges of any strong heat source, including volcanic eruptions and steam from power plants. Forest fires often create strong whirlwinds with tornado-like force. Similarly, during World War II, the bombing of Dresden, Germany, in February 1945 created a deadly firestorm that destroyed more than 8 square miles (21 square kilometers) of the city.

TERRIFYING TWISTERS

Unlike a whirlwind, the violently rotating winds that create a **tornado** start from the top down. The winds of a tornado reach outward like a vacuum cleaner nozzle from a passing storm front. Layers of spinning winds make up a tornado, each layer moving at a different speed. The fastest part of the tornado is the outer face of the funnel cloud, where the winds can reach speeds above 400 miles (644 kilometers) per hour.

As air masses clash over the Great Plains, they breed more tornadoes than anywhere else in the world—creating Tornado Alley, just east of the Rocky Mountains. But tornadoes can form anywhere. Tornadoes spin off from **thunderstorms**, especially violent thunderstorms created when warm, moist air is pushed eastward by a cold front. In Tornado Alley, these thunderstorms build along a dryline, a separation between warm, moist air and hot, dry air. Where air near the ground flows upward into higher terrain, such as in the front range of the Rocky Mountains, the flow of the wind frequently forms thunderstorms.

Within the thunderstorm clouds, surface air pushes upward. Since the winds within a thunderstorm can move at up to 100 miles (161 kilometers) per hour, this rising air sometimes takes on a spin, forming a wall cloud that hangs off the edge of the storm. The cloud tilts vertically, and the wind picks up speed, building a funnel cloud around a center of extremely low pressure, creating a tornado.

Tornadoes vary greatly in strength and speed. The weakest tornadoes are called **land spouts**, comprising 69 percent of all reported tornadoes. Like the weak **waterspouts** that form over water, these tornadoes last less than ten minutes and have wind speeds barely above those of the thunderstorm that generated them. Only 2 percent of all tornadoes are truly violent, causing the majority of deaths and injuries. The Fujita Intensity Scale measures the strength of a tornado; an F5 tornado —causing "incredible" damage—is the most destructive, with winds up to 318 miles (512 kilometers) per hour.

A tornado roars through a Texas field.

When a tornado touches down, it rips up the ground, sucking up dirt, dust, debris, and even the course of a stream into the funnel cloud, coloring it darker. It hisses and roars with the furious sound of a speeding freight train. Yet a tornado may exhibit quirky behavior—stripping a house of its furniture but leaving the house intact, picking up people and setting them on trees, and dropping cows unhurt gently into distant fields. But ground zero of a tornado is one of the most dangerous places on earth. Its winds are unpredictable and so is its path. Anything caught in a tornado can be shredded apart. Objects as small and light as pieces of straw can become deadly projectiles.

If a tornado threatens, the dark clouds overhead may take on an eerie green glow. Today's early warning systems can give only twenty minutes' notice against an impending tornado, which is just enough time for people to seek shelter. Experts suggest that people take cover in a small, windowless room (like a basement, bathroom, or closet) and cover their head with a mattress or blanket to avoid injury from flying debris.

THE FUJITA INTENSITY SCALE

Created in 1971 by Professor T. Theodore Fujita of the University of Chicago, the Fujita Intensity Scale classifies the intensity of a tornado by correlating the damage it does to an estimate of its wind speed.

CLASS	WIND SPEED		TYPE	DAMAGE
	MILES PER HOUR	KILOMETERS PER HOUR		
F0	less than 72	less than 116	Gale tornado	Light damage: chimneys damaged, tree branches broken, billboards damaged
F1	73–112	117–180	Moderate	Moderate damage: moving cars off highways, roof surfaces peeled off, mobile homes pushed off foundations or overturned
F2	113–157	181–253	Significant	Considerable damage: large trees snapped or uprooted, roofs torn off frame houses, boxcars overturned
F3	158–206	254–332	Severe	Severe damage: most trees in a forest uprooted, roofs torn off well-constructed houses, trains tipped over, heavy cars lifted off the ground and thrown
F4	207–260	333–418	Devastating	Devastating damage: well-constructed houses leveled, structures with weak foundations blown some distance, cars thrown, large missiles generated
F5	261–318	419–512	Incredible	Incredible damage: strong frame houses leveled off foundations and swept away, car-sized objects thrown more than 109 yards (100m), trees debarked

HORRIFIC HURRICANES

Hurricanes are storms of immense proportion, with winds of 74 miles (119 kilometers) per hour or more swirling around a perfectly calm center. The word "hurricane" comes from *huracán*, a Taíno word meaning "big blow." The native Caribbean Taíno culture vanished after Christopher Columbus reached the New World, but hurricane season remains a fact of life for the residents of the Caribbean.

Hurricanes occur worldwide, although they appear under different names. From the Chinese word for "big wind," a **typhoon** is a hurricane that develops over the North Pacific Ocean, where most of the world's hurricanes occur. These storms wreak havoc along the Asian coast, destroying homes, sinking ships, and killing thousands of people during storm surges. Hurricanes spin off the equator to hit Australia and radiate out of the Indian Ocean as **cyclones**, with winds and storm surges causing enormous damage to Bangladesh, East Pakistan, and India. Cyclones cause more death and destruction than any other storms on earth. During one single storm in 1970, more than 300,000 people died in Bangladesh, mostly due to the storm surge that flooded the sea-level country.

North America copes with hurricanes from June to November that form around low-pressure systems spinning counterclockwise off the African coast and follow the trade winds across the sea toward the Caribbean. As they pick up warm moist air, they grow. A **tropical depression** forms when the winds rotate at 38 miles (61 kilometers) per hour, showing equal pressure around the system. The depression becomes a **tropical storm** when the winds exceed 38 miles (61 kilometers) per hour, and a hurricane when the winds reach speeds of 74 miles (119 kilometers) per hour. The same hurricanes that tear through the Caribbean often slam the East Coast of the United States during hurricane season. States along the Gulf of Mexico and the Atlantic Ocean are particularly vulnerable, with Florida most prone to hurricane damage.

A hurricane can reach up to 6 miles (10 kilometers) high into the atmosphere, with winds that extend more than 600 hundred miles (966 kilometers) from the center. The strongest winds are in the eyewall, which circulates around a perfectly calm center, the eye of the storm. Within the eyewall is a chimney, drawing warm moist air from the ocean's surface. This air gathers strength as it rises, expanding under the low pressure at the center of the storm. As the air rises, it cools and sinks back in, dropping moisture into the hurricane, releasing more heat.

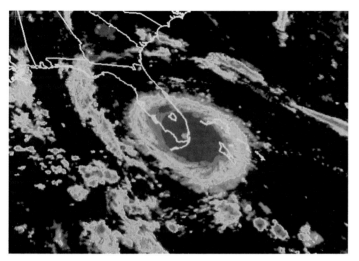

A radar image shows Hurricane Andrew engulfing the southern half of Florida's peninsula.

A zone of hurricane force winds surrounds the eyewall, driving narrow strips of clouds called rainbands, which drop heavy precipitation. The outer winds are gale-force winds, reaching from 20 to 60 miles (32 to 97 kilometers) from the eyewall to the edge of the storm, blowing at about 40 miles (64 kilometers) per hour. Along this outer edge, the right forward quadrant of a hurricane pushes a storm surge ahead of it, as the friction of strong winds on the ocean forces the sea level to rise.

In the United States, hurricane forecasts come from the National Oceanic and Atmospheric Administration (NOAA). Each year, this agency collects meteorological data and develops models to predict what each hurricane season will look like. In a "normal" hurricane year, forecasters predict eight to eleven tropical storms, five to seven of which will reach hurricane strength. Of these, two or three may become major hurricanes. In 2001, weather researchers from NOAA predicted that a climatic shift over the Atlantic Ocean (with water temperatures half a degree Fahrenheit higher than normal) would lead to more frequent, catastrophic hurricanes in the not-too-distant future.

When predicting the potential danger of an approaching hurricane, forecasters use the Saffir-Simpson Scale to determine whether coastal areas should be evacuated. Yet despite the immense amount of information available on which to base a prediction, hurricane forecasting is still an inexact science. A hurricane's path is difficult to predict. Air masses can deflect the hurricane from its original course. The winds may speed up or slow down as the storm moves over warm water or dry land.

Because of danger from the storm surge, flooding, and high winds, forecasters would rather err on the side of caution, encouraging evacuations. Thanks to the evacuation of more than two million people during Hurricane Andrew in 1992, only a few people died when the hurricane blew through South Florida with winds up to 177 miles (285 kilometers) per hour.

THE SAFFIR-SIMPSON SCALE	CATEGORY	WIND SPEED		DAMAGE
		MILES PER HOUR	KILOMETERS PER HOUR	
Developed in 1969 by Herbert Saffir, an engineer, and Dr. Robert Simpson, director of the National Hurricane Center, this five-point scale categorizes hurricanes by the relationship between their wind speed, their storm surge, and the damage done. Only two category 5 storms have reached the United States in the past century—the 1935 Florida Keys hurricane and Hurricane Camille in 1969. Although Hurricane Andrew in 1992 was a category 4 hurricane, it caused more than $38 billion dollars in damage to South Florida.	1	74–95	119–153	Damage to unanchored mobile homes, shrubs, and trees. Some coastal road flooding and minor pier damage.
	2	96–110	154–177	Considerable damage to mobile homes, piers, and vegetation. Coastal escape routes flood two to four hours before arrival of hurricane center. Buildings sustain roofing material, door, and window damage. Small boats in unprotected moorings break free.
	3	111–130	178–209	Mobile homes destroyed. Some structural damage to small homes and utility buildings. Flooding near coast destroys small structures. Terrain below 5 feet (2m) above sea level may flood up to 6 miles (9.7 km) inland.
	4	131–155	210–249	Extensive curtain wall failures with complete roof structure failure on small residences. Major erosion of beaches. Major damage to lower floors of structures near the shore. Terrain below 10 feet (3m) above sea level may flood up to 6 miles (9.7 km) inland, possibly requiring mass evacuations.
	5	Over 155	Over 249	Complete roof failure on many homes and industrial buildings. Some complete building failures. Major damage to lower floors of structures located less than 15 feet (5m) above sea level and within 500 yards (457m) of the shoreline. Massive evacuation of low ground residential areas may be required.

5
WICKED WINDS

On a summer day in 1999 at Chatham, Massachusetts, thirteen-year-old Jeffrey Plumer folded up his sails after an afternoon of sailing on Oyster Pond. Jeffrey was ready to head for home, but the wind had other ideas. As a wall of thunderstorm clouds moved toward the pond, it spun off a funnel cloud—and lifted Jeffrey and his boat out into the middle of the pond, about 200 yards (182 meters).

Rescuers could hardly believe Jeffrey's story, but a man kayaking on Oyster Pond confirmed it.

EXPLOSIVE BURSTS

The wind that dumped Jeffrey in the lake was a **gustnado**, not a tornado—one of several classifications of severely strong but brief gusts of wind. Winds driven by thunderstorm cells can sometimes reach proportions that are almost, but not quite, tornadoes. The gustnado forms when vigorous downdrafts from the top of a thunderstorm collide with winds blowing in different directions from outside the thunderstorm, forming a brief whirling gust that can reach speeds of more than 70 miles (113 kilometers) per hour.

Another sudden downward movement of wind is the **microburst**. Like a landslide of wind, a microburst collapses downward from higher altitudes to lower in a pillarlike formation, forcing wind to crash against the ground with intense force. In the dry southwestern United States, one of

A gustnado is a severely strong but brief gust of wind.

the driving forces behind a microburst is verga—rain that evaporates from clouds before hitting the ground. The evaporation creates cool heavy air that drops down suddenly, picking up speed as it hits the ground. The explosive force of a microburst is enough to slam a plane out of the sky or to flip over a plane parked on a runway.

A microburst is a type of **wind shear**, which is a sharp change in wind speed or direction over a short distance. The change can occur vertically, as in a microburst, or horizontally. Wind shear typically happens at the edge of a storm front or over a mountain range.

THE NOT-SO-FRIENDLY SKIES

Clouds are often a clue to turbulence in the stratosphere. But pilots know that turbulence can strike out of perfectly clear air. On December 28, 1997, United Airlines Flight 826 left Tokyo for Honolulu, cruising above 30,000 feet (9,144 meters) in clear air. Suddenly, the plane began to shake, then plunged a hundred feet. The oxygen masks popped out, and passengers without seatbelts were flung across the cabin. Eighty-three people were injured, and one person died.

Wind shear typically happens at the edge of a storm front and can easily flip a plane.

As part of their training, airline pilots learn to recover the plane during clear air turbulence, where invisible **vortexes** of wind spin off jet streams. But how can pilots anticipate something they can't see on their radar screen? At the National Center for Atmospheric Research (NCAR) and National Aeronautics and Space Administration (NASA) Dryden Flight Research Center, researchers use lasers to detect turbulence in a project called LIDAR. A laser mounted on the nose of an aircraft sends out a certain frequency of light. Tiny, invisible-to-the-human-eye dust particles in the atmosphere allow the light to be reflected back. If the path of the light changes, the pilot can tell that invisible turbulence is ahead.

Clouds help to identify some wind vortices in the troposphere, such as **von Karmen vortices**. These formations occur when a stable atmosphere with low clouds flows past an obstacle (often a mountain) whose height is greater than the depth of the cloud layer. The air movement around the obstacle produces eddies in the wake of a cloud layer, like the patterns of water flowing over rocks in a stream.

UPS AND DOWNS

Within the violent winds of a thunderstorm, updrafts and downdrafts lift and drop columns of air just like an elevator. Thunderstorm clouds can be divided into cells based on the behavior of the winds within the clouds. Each cell has an updraft, a column of ascending warm air, and a downdraft, a column of descending cool air—like two adjoining elevators. The updraft may first rise at about 20 miles (32 kilometers) per hour, but as the cell gains intensity, the wind speed of the updraft can reach as high as 150 miles (241 kilometers) per hour. Behind the updraft, the downdraft carries the chilled winds back down, usually at speeds of 20 to 30 miles (32 to 48 kilometers) per hour. When the downdraft hits the ground, it bursts outward, forcing strong gusts of wind in every direction.

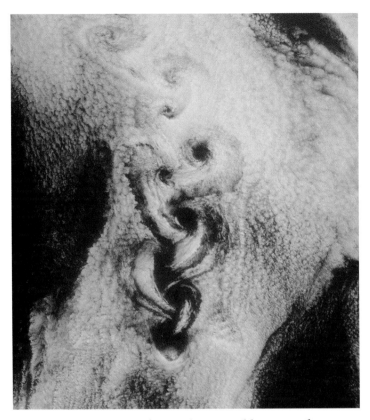

Von Karmen vortices form when a stable atmosphere with low clouds flows past a relatively small obstacle with a height greater than the depth of the cloud layer.

Thunderstorm winds are dangerous because of their unpredictability. The updraft and downdraft columns move around within the cell, creating violent whirlwinds and eddies that can tear apart an aircraft. This dance of winds can spawn tornadoes and create tremendous **thundersqualls**— strong winds that blow out of the downdraft and push ahead of the storm, gusting up to 100 miles (161 kilometers) per hour.

Thunderstorms lose their steam when the downdraft becomes stronger than the updraft. As it gathers and drops moisture, the width of the down-

EXTRATERRESTRIAL WINDS

In the depths of space, a different sort of wind moves—the **solar wind**. Born from explosive ejections of matter from the sun, streamers of electrically charged particles race across space, creating auroras in our Northern Hemisphere and interrupting satellite and radio communications with electromagnetic impulses.

Earth is not the only planet in our solar system to experience winds. Space probes have captured images of storm winds on Saturn and dust devils on Mars. Jupiter's Red Spot is the largest known storm in our solar system, first noticed by astronomers 300 years ago. The Red Spot behaves like a cyclone, rotating counterclockwise. Winds within the storm blow at speeds of up to 270 miles (435 kilometers) per hour.

Swirling, stormlike features possibly associated with wind shear can be seen near Jupiter's Great Red Spot (GRS).

draft expands, cutting off the updraft. With no further fuel carried upward to feed the storm, the winds die down.

CROSSWINDS

On July 1, 1940, the Tacoma Narrows Bridge opened in Washington, linking the Olympic Peninsula with Tacoma. As motorists drove across the span, 2,800 feet (853 meters) long, the bridge bounced. It wasn't an ordinary bounce, though—it was more like a wave that flowed along the entire length of the bridge, raising the roadway 3 feet (1 meter). Cars in front would disappear from view as the bridge rose up and down. Because of this unusual behavior, the Tacoma Narrows Bridge soon received the nickname Galloping Gertie and became a tourist attraction, although many motorists avoided the bridge completely as this wasn't how a bridge was supposed to act!

Four months after it opened, on November 7, the bridge started bucking and kicking in a wind blowing at 40 miles (64 kilometers) per hour. A cable band broke. Officials closed the bridge to traffic, and as engineers, scientists, and reporters watched, the roadway twisted and rocked in rhythm with the wind until a 600-foot (183-meter)-long section of the bridge broke off and fell into the water below. With this dramatic ending caught on film, Galloping Gertie became a model for all civil engineers on how *not* to design a bridge.

Bridges are particularly sensitive to lateral winds that blow through an enclosed space, such as a deep river valley. Road signs warn motorists of **crosswinds**, because the lateral winds blowing across the width of a bridge can push a car into oncoming traffic. These winds are generally orographic winds, constantly flowing down a tight passage, gathering speed as the space constricts. Lateral winds can also drive sailing ships against reefs or rocks in a narrow passage.

6
WINDS, CLIMATE, AND WEATHER

Wind drives weather, and weather influences wind. When a high-pressure area moves into a region, it brings uncomplicated weather—hot and dry summer days, cold and clear winter days. But air at high pressure always moves toward an area of low pressure. And a low-pressure system overhead means stormy skies.

ALL UP FRONT

When the wind starts to propel an air mass across the planet, the weather below the air mass changes. Arctic air pushed down from Canada across the Great Plains means that ground temperatures will drop to bitter extremes. Caribbean air pushed up the Mississippi River brings wet, warm weather. Since winds are pushing air masses all over the place, the air masses constantly battle with each other, meeting at an edge called a front.

When a warm front rolls through, the lighter warm air rises over the heavier cold air. The warm air slowly condenses, creating rain clouds that might drop their loads behind the warm front.

A cold front happens when a mass of heavy cold air wedges itself under a mass of lighter warm air. As the warm air is quickly forced upward, it cools and condenses, forming rain. The leading edge of a cold front produces the roughest weather. Cold fronts often develop a squall line—a line of thunderstorms that can be hundreds of miles long and a few miles wide, traveling many miles ahead of the front, announcing its advance.

A cloud bank marks the surface of a cold front as a relatively cold air mass moves in, lifting lighter, warmer air and causing condensation of moisture as the warm air increases in altitude and condenses.

A stationary front happens when a cold front and a warm front meet, but neither one wins. Unpleasant weather can occur at the boundary as the masses of air push against one another. Sometimes, the air starts to mix together, forming a single air mass called an occlusion.

CREATING CLIMATE

The constant interaction of air masses, high-pressure systems, and low-pressure systems drives the earth's weather. But wind shapes climate as well. Climate is the predictable behavior of weather in a certain region. A

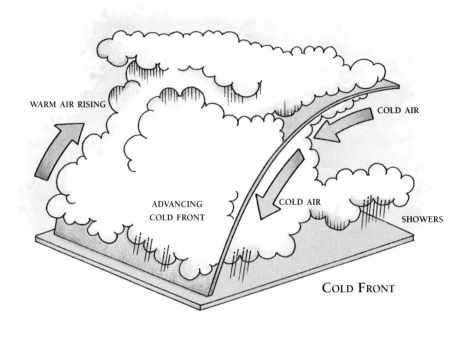

WARM AIR RISING

COLD AIR

ADVANCING
COLD FRONT

COLD AIR

SHOWERS

COLD FRONT

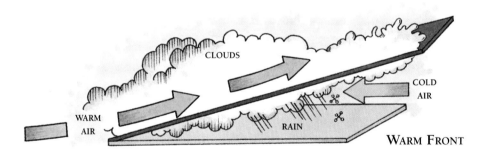

CLOUDS

COLD
AIR

WARM
AIR

RAIN

WARM FRONT

desert will be hot and dry. The polar regions are cold and dry. Equatorial rain forests are warm and wet.

Permanent high-pressure and low-pressure systems contribute to climate. The bands of winds that circle our planet directly affect the earth's surface below them. At the equator, permanent low-pressure systems generate rain. At the poles, permanent low-pressure systems cause arid conditions.

Prevailing winds can also shape climate. In the cold, dry tundra, wind defines an arid climate. Wildflowers clinging to the alpine tundra rarely grow more than a few inches tall, so they can tolerate the wind speed of 3 miles (5 kilometers) per hour that ruffles their leaves. Yet just 3 feet (1 meter) above the surface, the wind can be howling past at 30 miles (48 kilometers) per hour.

Winds and water interact to form climates. Winds blowing over the Gulf Stream, a stream of warm water flowing clockwise around the Atlantic Ocean, makes Great Britain's climate generally warm and damp—even though the islands lie at the same latitude as icy Labrador, in Canada's Maritime Provinces. During the winter months, cold air collides with the warm waters of the Gulf Stream off the coast of New England, breeding nor'easters.

GRAIN BY GRAIN

Wind is a powerful force of erosion. It changes the landscape grain by grain as it sweeps sand, dust, dirt, and microscopic particles across surfaces, smoothing and polishing the edges of rocks, abrading and removing rough material. In the desert, winds create **sandstorms** and scour desert rocks with blowing sand, eroding them into arches and unusual shapes.

In the desert and on the shore, wind defines the landscape as it shifts sand into new and different patterns as sand dunes. Dunes build up grain by grain around the smallest of anchors—a rock, a shell, or a blade of grass. Even when a dune stabilizes, it continues to move in the direction toward which the wind is blowing, shifting shape at the whim of the wind.

When the wind carries and deposits dust across a large area, it creates a dense, mineral-rich soil called loess. Much of southern China's farmland is loess that blew in from the Gobi Desert, creating deposits up to 1,000 feet (305 meters) thick! In Wisconsin and southern Iowa, loess provides the world's most productive soil for growing wheat, corn, and soybeans.

Wind erosion can be a serious problem for farmers. After many years of drought and damage from plowing, the flat prairie farmlands of Texas, Oklahoma, Kansas, and Colorado started to blow away in 1935. Massive clouds of dust drifted as far as the Atlantic Ocean, raining down soil on ships 300 miles (483 kilometers) out to sea.

SPIN OF THE SEASON

As the seasons change, so do the winds *and* the weather. Over the Atlantic Ocean, hurricane season comes like clockwork every year, when wind patterns shift in early June. When the monsoon over Asia shifts, it changes the weather patterns from clear and dry to very wet. We associate the word monsoon with rain, since the monsoon wind brings extreme moisture in the summer after a period of extreme dryness in the winter. Asian rivers swell to immense proportions during the monsoon season. Bangladesh, sitting on the world's largest delta between the immense Ganges and Hugli rivers, is the world's most flood-prone country. Nearly a fifth of its land disappears under water during the monsoon.

There are two distinct Asian monsoons. One occurs in southern Asia, fueled by the interaction between the Indian subcontinent, the Arabian Sea, and the Indian Ocean. The other is the East Asia monsoon, the inter-

A blizzard hits North Kingstown in Rhode Island.

action of coastal China and Japan with the surrounding waters of the Pacific Ocean. Cyclones are born during the period in which the monsoon shifts, when dry winds flowing away from the coastline struggle with wet winds attempting to push inland.

OCEANS IN MOTION

In addition to the Gulf Stream and other fixed-position flows of ocean water that affect the world's winds, warm and cold pools of water drift back and forth across the oceans. As the wind drives the waves, the waves move the water. Called oscillations, these water movements dramatically affect the earth's weather, including the flow of winds.

Although oscillations occur in both the North Atlantic and the North Pacific, the most famous oscillation is the *El Niño/La Niña* effect in the South Pacific, affecting much of the Southern Hemisphere. Every three to seven years, the normal trade winds in the South Pacific relax a little, allowing a warm pool of water in the western Pacific to drift along the equator toward South America. The warm water shuts off the cooler waters that attract fish to the coast of Peru and brings torrential rains to an otherwise arid land. Called *El Niño* (Spanish for "the Christ child") because of its appearance in late December, its effects reach from the Pacific Rim to eastern Africa, bringing heavy rain to places that usually receive little rain and affecting the behavior of the Asian monsoons.

THE WINDCHILL

When temperatures drop and the wind increases, humans become susceptible to windchill—the way the wind feels in cold weather. An Antarctic explorer, Paul Siple, developed a method of measuring windchill in 1939. Windchill is expressed as a temperature that is lower than the actual temperature of the air depending on the wind speed. As the windchill drops, more calories of heat are whisked away from exposed skin. A temperature of 20°F (-7°C) in a wind blowing at 35 miles (56 kilometers) per hour feels the same as –20°F (–29°C). Adding your own movement to the wind's effect by running, skiing, or snowmobiling makes the windchill even more severe. Below –20°F (–29°C), skin becomes frostbitten rapidly. Below –70°F (–57°C), skin freezes within thirty seconds. When enjoying winter sports, be sure to take the windchill into account, and bundle up!

WINDS AND SNOW

When the wind kicks up above 35 miles (56 kilometers) per hour during a snowstorm, a **blizzard** happens. The roaring wind raises clouds of dry, light snowflakes into the air. Just like a sandstorm in the desert, a blizzard blots out visibility, causing a whiteout that can last for days.

Buffalo, Rochester, Cleveland, and many other cities in the northern United States regularly receive unusually large amounts of snow during the winter months, thanks to the interaction of wind with the vast watery surfaces of the Great Lakes. Lake effect snow happens when Arctic winds blow southeasterly across the Great Lakes, plucking up moisture from the surface of the lake and depositing it as snow. In 1977, the city of Buffalo disappeared for eleven days under the snowdrifts brought on by a blizzard off Lake Erie. Snow piled up to the roofs of houses, and reindeer escaped from the Buffalo Zoo by walking right over the fence and out of their pen! During December 2001, Buffalo disappeared under snowdrifts again as more than 5 feet (1.5 meters) of snow fell in five days. Two weeks after the storm ended, the city was still clearing the streets, trucking away snow to nearby dump sites. Rochester asked to "borrow" some of Buffalo's snow for its winter festival since the snow piles at the dumpsites in Buffalo rose up to 200 feet (61 meters) high.

Residents of Alaska and the Canadian plains often see snow rollers, downy white jelly-roll-shaped formations of snow in an otherwise untouched field. When fluffy snow falls on a layer of ice or packed snow, and temperatures are close to freezing, high winds can pick up the new snow, forming perfect layers that roll along with the wind, much as a person would roll a giant snowball for a snowman.

Wind also causes Aeolian ice lenses to form in certain desert environments during the winter. When winter storms hit, snowdrifts form on the leeward side of each dune. Wind pushes the sand over the snow, trapping it inside the dune, insulating it from the sun. As the weather warms up, these ice lenses slowly melt, providing a steady source of moisture to plants during the spring and summer.

LIVING WITH WINDS

It is harvest time in Tibet, time for families to cut barley from the fields and prepare it for use in their traditional food, *tsampa*. To remove the kernels of barley, the dried stalks of grain are beaten, or threshed, on the roofs of houses. The rhythm of the harvest has remained the same for thousands of years. In the village of Bitu, Wade Brackenbury, an American traveler, watched:

"The threshing was done by groups of three, who sang as they worked. They would sweep the barley into baskets, to be sifted in the wind. Whoever was sifting whistled for the wind to come, and as soon as he whistled, a long, gentle gust would come along and carry the chaff away. When one scoop of barley was done, the wind would die down again. Then they would get the next scoop, whistle for the wind to come again, and it would. I watched one girl, about 12 years old, do this for an hour, and the wind came every time she whistled."

HARNESSING THE WIND

Wind has always played an important role in people's lives. Like the Tibetans, many of us rely on the wind to help us with our daily work, great and small. From ancient times, threshing floors relied on the power of wind to separate the heavy, useful grain from the lighter and useless chaff, the inedible part of the plant.

This wind farm at Palm Springs, California, features a "forest" of wind turbines.

It wasn't until the eleventh century A.D. that people actively harnessed the power of the wind. Then the first windmills appeared on the islands of Greece and in the Middle East. These windmills provided a mechanized way to thresh grain, separating the edible kernels from the useless chaff and grinding the kernels into flour. By the 1400s, windmills constructed in the Netherlands pumped water out of marshes, creating dry farmland. After pioneers settled the western United States, windmills sprouted on the prairies and the vast, dry expanses of cattle ranches, drawing drinking water from deep within the ground.

Although windmills are still used for these purposes today, the idea of using a windmill to generate electricity first caught on in the 1930s, before rural parts of the United States were electrified. The concept of large-scale wind farming took hold in the 1970s. With wind turbines—modern windmills with sails that look like giant propellers—in places where winds blow strongly all year long, electricity can be generated by the power of a constant wind turning the sails. Using wind farms stationed on windswept hilltops in Texas and Colorado, one of the world's largest wind-powered facilities generates enough electricity to light 139,000 homes. Wind-powered generation is clean and green, saving dwindling supplies of fossil fuels—and the wind is free for the taking. Experts claim that wind power could fulfill 20 percent of the United States's electricity needs by the year 2020.

GOING WITH THE FLOW

No one knows who invented the first sailing ship, but the Phoenicians, who lived 2,500 years ago along the shores of what is now Syria and Lebanon, built sailing ships for commerce and sold ships to other countries. The word "sail" became synonymous with the movement of a ship. The era of the great sailing ships lasted for centuries. Using knowledge of

Wherever winds blow across bodies of water, today's adventurers find ways to capture and enjoy it.

the winds, adventurous captains like Christopher Columbus and Vasco da Gama led their crews across the wide, unknown oceans to distant continents. Ships evolved from square-sailed, single-masted vessels to clipper ships with three masts and an array of different sails for different purposes, with the most intricate designs developed between 1840 and 1905.

Once oceangoing steamships appeared in the early 1800s, the days of the grand sailing ship were numbered. Commercial traffic shifted to steamships and diesel-powered ships. With sailing ships no longer the driving force of world commerce, sailing became a sport—and a very popular one. Oceangoing sailors still ride the trade winds between the Mediterranean and the Caribbean, clustering in tropical ports during the winter months. All along the East Coast of the United States, sailboats ply the Atlantic Ocean and its many bays, benefiting from ideal winds for sailing. Inland sailors enjoy the challenge of skimming across a lake, sails unfurled. Clipper ships still sail, but their cargo is tourists as they run the old trade routes of the Caribbean and the Atlantic coast.

ADRIFT IN AIR

Adapted to use the wind and its currents, birds and bats have hollow bones like honeycombs, allowing them to float on the breeze. Studying how an albatross flew, a sailor from Brittany, Captain Jean-Marie le Bris, invented the glider in 1855. Unlike mythological Icarus, who attempted to fly by attaching birds' feathers to his arms, le Bris relied on the craft being towed until it caught the wind. Many birds take advantage of a **thermal**, a rising current of warm air, to quickly gain altitude. Thermals rise above small slopes and up along the sides of cliffs. The glider, a plane without an engine, uses thermals to rise high into the atmosphere and drift. Gliders are used for recreation rather than transportation. Now towed by a powered aircraft high into the sky, the glider detaches. The pilot finds thermals to ride, floating as silently as a hawk across the sky.

Just like birds, gliders and airplanes float on air, thanks to the Bernoulli principle. Airplane wings have curved tops and straight undersides. The air flowing over a wing moves at a higher speed than the air under the wing, so it is at a lower pressure. It also has to travel a longer distance than the air under the wing. Because of high pressure below the wing and low pressure above the wing, the wing constantly pushes up, keeping the plane in the air.

A glider uses thermals to rise high into the atmosphere.

Aircraft are designed to work with the winds. Airline timetables reflect a difference in travel time depending on whether a plane is going east or west—a westbound flight is always faster, thanks to the persistent westerlies. Commercial aircraft fly in the stratosphere not just to avoid weather and turbulence, but also to take advantage of the winds. **Tailwinds** propel aircraft at a higher speed, pushing the plane from behind within the flow of a westerly or in the jet stream. **Head winds** act like an obstacle, forcing the plane to burn up more fuel as it pushes against the wind. The same

LET'S GO FLY A KITE

Children and adults around the world share in playing with the wind when they fly kites. In some parts of Asia, musical kites play a tune as the wind whistles through reeds or bamboo attached to the kite. Boys in India fight aerial battles, swooping and twirling their kites in order to cut through each other's kite strings. Many countries celebrate kite-flying days. China has Kite-flying Day on the ninth day of the ninth month of the year. Thousands of kites take to the air as families in Greece celebrate Clean Monday, forty days before Easter Sunday.

But kites weren't always for fun. In addition to carrying meteorological instruments to great heights and serving as a science experiment for Benjamin Franklin in 1762, kites have been used for warfare. During the Spanish-American War, Americans sent cameras up on kites to take aerial photos of troop movements. Kites were adapted to carry a person, leading to hang gliding—used by the Germans to spy on coastlines during World War II.

Kite flying is a popular activity throughout the world.

holds true at ground level. Sailors, motorists, bicyclists, and runners notice the effects of tailwinds and head winds.

RESPECTING THE WIND

With lessons learned from engineering mistakes such as Galloping Gertie, engineers and architects incorporate respect for the wind into their designs. In 1998, Japanese engineers designed the world's longest suspension bridge, 12,828 feet (3,910 meters) across the Akashi Strait from Kobe to Honshu. To cope with the frequent gale-force winds that tear through the strait, the engineers designed dampers inside each bridge tower. These dampers sway in the opposite direction of the wind, canceling out the effect of the wind against the bridge deck. With this special design, engi-

The social and economic costs of a devastating hurricane can be immense.

neers expect the bridge to endure winds of up to 180 miles (290 kilometers) per hour. The bridge is also designed to withstand earthquakes.

Skyscrapers must be designed to move with the wind, to prevent wind damage. In the windy city of Chicago, the Sears Tower can sway as much as 10 inches (25.4 centimeters) in any direction, moving along with the wind rather than standing firm against it. Buildings within hurricane-prone regions must meet certain criteria to protect their occupants, such as the roof being designed in such a way that the Bernoulli effect of a storm doesn't tear it off. In 2000, Louisiana State University established the world's first hurricane engineering curriculum, intended to train new architects and engineers not just to build better buildings, but to understand the social costs to communities when hurricanes strike.

Since 1871, engineers have used wind tunnels in the laboratory to simulate certain airflow conditions over buildings and vehicles. In the wind tunnel, they can generate wind at certain speeds, air pressures, and temperatures. Today, computer simulations of airflow have become more common. In planning a new airport for Hong Kong, scientists worked with architects to develop computer models of the interaction between wind and landscape in order to determine where *not* to place the runways. These intricate computer models of wind behavior can take a month to process on the world's fastest computers, but their value is incalculable. By using models, architects can design buildings that can better withstand dangerous winds, particularly hurricanes and cyclones.

Designers of cars, especially race cars, also work with the wind. After studying the dynamics of airflow around their intended design, engineers shape the car body to minimize friction. On the back of a car, a wind foil reduces the amount of friction by channeling the wind away from the body of the car. On sports cars and race cars, hood-mounted scoops force wind into the engine, increasing its ability to transform fuel into power.

Without the wind, the earth would be a barren place, unsuitable for life. Although many winds cause problems for human civilization, the winds themselves simply are. Along with the other residents of planet Earth, we have learned to live with the winds, to use the winds, to respect the winds.

adiabatic: warm downslope winds

Aeolian ice lenses: slow-melting snowdrifts buried in sand by strong winds

Aeolian sounds: haunting sounds made by the wind as it flows over and around an obstacle, creating eddies of air

air mass: a large cohesive body of air that derives its temperature from the land or water below it

air pressure: the difference in the density of molecules as air is heated and cooled

Bernoulli principle: the principle that a fluid (such as air) in motion is at a lower pressure than a stationary fluid and will draw the stationary fluid toward it to equalize the pressure

blizzard: winds of 35 miles (56 kilometers) per hour or more during a snow-storm, causing poor to no visibility

bora: a cold wind flowing from the Hungarian basin to the Adriatic Sea

circulation cell: large areas of air movement created by the rotation of the earth and the interaction of winds between the equator and the poles

clear air turbulence: atmospheric turbulence occurring under tranquil, cloud-less conditions, subjecting aircraft to sudden updrafts and downdrafts

climate: the predictable weather patterns that occur in a certain region

conduction: heat transfer between molecules, with heat flowing from an area of high temperature to an area of low temperature

convection: heat transfer in a fluid, such as air, caused by differences in density and the action of gravity

Coriolis force: effect of the earth's rotation that causes water and wind to spin counterclockwise north of the equator and clockwise south of the equator

crosswind: a lateral wind

cyclone: winds around any low-pressure system, where the air spirals inward to the center, then pushes upward; synonym for "hurricane" in the Indian Ocean

doldrums: a narrow zone of almost no wind near the equator

downdraft: a column of descending cool air within a thunderstorm

downslope winds: another term for katabatic winds

dryline: separation of warm, moist air to the east from hot, dry air to the west, causing thunderstorms to form

dust devil: a small, strong whirlwind, visible because it picks up dirt and dust

dust whirl: a little whirlwind

easterlies: persistent winds with an easterly trend

episodic winds: winds that occur seasonally

eye: the calm center of a hurricane

eyewall: the tight cylinder of a hurricane's strongest winds, centered around the eye

foehn: a warm, dry wind flowing down the leeward side of a mountain range

front: the boundary line between two dissimilar air masses

funnel cloud: a violent, rotating column of air that doesn't touch the ground

gale: continuous winds blowing stronger than a breeze, from more than 12 miles (19 kilometers) per hour up to hurricane-force winds of 74 miles (119 kilometers) per hour

gust: a sudden, short blast of gale-force winds

gustnado: a whirling hurricane-force gust of wind ejected by a thunderstorm

haboob: Sudanese name for a dust storm or sandstorm that forms a moving cloud

head wind: a wind blowing in the opposite direction from a moving object, impeding its progress

high-pressure system: an area where the atmospheric pressure exceeds 1,013.2 millibars

horse latitudes: a calm high-pressure area in the North Atlantic between the trade winds and the westerlies

hurricane: an immense low-pressure system circulating around a perfectly calm center, with winds exceeding 74 miles (119 kilometers) per hour

jet stream: streams of rapidly moving air that flow west at altitudes between 30,000 and 45,000 feet (9,100 to 13,700 meters)

katabatic winds: cold, dense winds pulled downhill by gravity

koembang: a foehn that blows across Java

lake effect: the effect of a lake in modifying the weather around it

land breezes: a coastal wind that blows from land to sea created when the temperature of the sea is warmer than the land

land spout: a weak tornado that churns up soil

lateral wind: a wind blowing perpendicular to an object

leeward: the side sheltered from the wind

levant: a persistent wet easterly wind in the Adriatic Sea

low-pressure system: an area where the atmospheric pressure is below 1,000 millibars

maestro: a northwesterly wind bringing good weather to the Adriatic coast

meltemi: a summer wind that blows across the Mediterranean Sea

microburst: a severe downward burst of wind from a thunderstorm

mistral: a cold, dry wind blowing from the north across the Mediterranean Sea

monsoon: any seasonal wind that blows toward a continent for half the year and away from it for the other half

nor'easter: a winter cyclone occurring off the eastern coast of North America

norther: a cold, strong wind pushing Arctic air across the Great Plains of North America

orographic: localized winds that derive their character from the landscape

persistent winds: winds that blow in a regular direction on a regular basis

polar easterlies: moderate easterly winds located between the poles and the nearest low-pressure belt

sandstorm: wind-driven sand, moving in clouds at high speeds

Santa Ana: a foehn that flows off the Santa Ana mountains in California

sea breezes: a coastal wind that blows from sea to land, created when the temperature of the land is warmer than the sea

sirocco: a warm wind across the Mediterranean Sea, often blowing from the Sahara Desert

snow roller: a snowball-like formation created by wind

solar wind: a stream of electrically charged particles emitted by the sun

storm surge: coastal flooding created by a rise in sea level caused by the strong right forward quadrant winds of a hurricane

tailwind: a wind blowing in the same direction as a moving object, assisting its progress

thermal: a rising column of warm air

thundersquall: a brief, sudden windstorm, accompanied by thunder and lightning

thunderstorm: a localized storm with lightning and thunder, often accompanied by rain, heavy winds, and hail

tornado: a violently rotating column of air that touches the ground

trade winds: winds that flow easterly toward regions of low pressure near the equator

transmountain winds: winds that lose their moisture as they flow over a mountain

tropical depression: a low-pressure system circulating around a calm center, with winds up to 38 miles (61 kilometers) per hour

tropical storm: a low-pressure system circulating around a calm center, with winds between 39 and 73 miles (62 and 118 kilometers) per hour

turbulence: irregular motions of air, caused by random fluctuations in the wind flow

typhoon: a tropical cyclone that takes shape over the North Pacific Ocean

updraft: a column of ascending warm air within a thunderstorm

verga: wisps of rain that evaporate before hitting the ground

von Karmen vortices: eddies in the wind, noticeable in a cloud layer when a cloud-bearing wind pushes past a promontory, such as a mountain

vortex: a swirl of wind

wall cloud: an abrupt lowering of a cloud below its parent cloud, typically during a thunderstorm

waterspout: a tornado over water

westerlies: the dominant east-to-west motion of the atmospheric winds across the middle latitudes of both hemispheres

whirlwind: a rising, swirling column of wind caused by convection

willy-willy: Australian term for dust devil

windchill: the cooling of the human body caused by the motion of the air

wind shear: a sharp change in wind speed or direction over a short distance

windward: the side affected by the wind

zonda: a hot, sultry wind that pushes tropical air from the north across Argentina and Uruguay

FURTHER READING

Bortz, Fred, with J. Marshall Shepherd. *Dr. Fred's Weather Watch: Create and Run Your Own Weather Station.* New York: McGraw-Hill, 2000.

Branley, Franklyn Mansfield, and Giulio Maestro. *Tornado Alert.* New York: HarperTrophy, 1990.

Downs, Sandra Friend. *Shaping the Earth: Erosion.* Brookfield, CT: Twenty-First Century Books, 2000.

Lampton, Christopher F. *Hurricane.* Brookfield, CT: The Millbrook Press, 1994.

Morris, Neil. *Hurricanes & Tornadoes.* New York: Crabtree Publishing, 1998.

Murphy, Jim. *Blizzard: The Storm That Changed America.* New York: Scholastic, 2000.

Simon, Seymour. *Storms.* New York: Mulberry Books, 1992.

———. *Tornadoes.* New York: Morrow Junior, 1999.

———. *Weather.* New York: HarperCollins, 2000.

Vogel, Carole Garbuny. *Nature's Fury: Eyewitness Reports of Natural Disasters.* New York: Scholastic, 2000.

ON THE WORLD WIDE WEB
The Internet is always growing and changing, so you never know where you'll find the next cool site on wind! Use these Web sites as a starting point, and try your favorite search engine with keywords like "wind," "hurricane," "tornado," "blizzard," and "weather" to find more information on our earth's wild winds.

El Niño: Hot Air Over Hot Water
sln.fi.edu/weather/nino/indes.html
This Web site describes the how and why of *El Niño*.

Hurricanes: A Fierce Force of Nature
observe.ivv.nasa.gov/nasa/earth/hurricane/splash.html
An interactive Web site that explains how and where hurricanes form.

Hurricane Hunters
www.hurricanehunters.com/
The United States's official hurricane hunters, the 53rd Weather Reconnaissance Squadron of the Air Force Reserve send back photos from the eye of the storm!

Names of Winds
www.ggweather.com/winds.html
A list of unusual and interesting names and types of winds around the world.

The National Hurricane Center
www.nhc.noaa.gov/
The United States's primary resource for hurricane information.

Tornado and Storm Research Organisation
www.torro.org.uk/
This research Web site covers twisters in Europe.

Tornado Chase Day
www.chaseday.com/chaseday5.htm
Use this professional photographer's up-close views of tornadoes and other dangerous winds to identify the many different types of tornadoes.

The Tornado Project Online
www.tornadoproject.com/
Everything you wanted to know about tornadoes.

Whirling Winds of the World
freespace.virgin.net/mike.ryding/
Categorizing the earth's winds as global, seasonal, local, or spinning, this Web site gives an explanation (and sometimes a photo) of each type of wind.

Wind Chill Home Page
observe.ivv.nasa.gov/nasa/earth/wind_chill/chill_home.html
From NASA's Observatorium, this Web site explains why windchill occurs and provides calculators so you can determine the windchill outside.

Wind Engineering Research Center
www.wind.ttu.edu/mainpage.htm
This Web site presents scholarly information on wind energy, wind engineering, storms, and storm safety, including special sections for kids and teachers.

ABOUT THE AUTHOR

Sandra Friend is the author of many books for young adults, including *Florida in the Civil War: A State in Turmoil* (Millbrook) and the other books in Millbrook's **Exploring Planet Earth** series. She lives in Florida, where she enjoys hiking, canoeing, and kayaking along the windswept beaches of the Atlantic, just 40 miles away.